Spot Illustrations
from Women's Magazines
of the Teens and Twenties

828 Cuts
of Women, Family,
Home, Garden, etc.

Compiled and Arranged
by
JUDY M. JOHNSON

Dover Publications, Inc.
New York

Copyright © 1989 by Dover Publications, Inc.

All rights reserved under Pan American and International Copyright Conventions.

Published in Canada by General Publishing Company, Ltd., 30 Lesmill Road, Don Mills, Toronto, Ontario.

Spot Illustrations from Women's Magazines of the Teens and Twenties: 828 Cuts of Women, Family, Home, Garden, etc. is a new work, first published by Dover Publications, Inc., in 1989.

DOVER *Pictorial Archive* SERIES

Manufactured in the United States of America
Dover Publications, Inc., 31 East 2nd Street, Mineola, N.Y. 11501

Library of Congress Cataloging-in-Publication Data

Spot illustrations from women's magazines of the teens and twenties : 828 cuts
   of women, family, home, garden, etc. / compiled and arranged by Judy M.
   Johnson.
      p.   cm. — (Pictorial archive series)
   ISBN 0-486-26116-6
    1. Magazine illustration—20th century—United States—Themes, motives.
  2. Women's periodicals—Illustrations—Themes, motives. I. Johnson, Judy M.
  II. Series: Dover pictorial archive series.
NC975.S7   1989
741.6′52—dc20   89-33496
                                              CIP

Introduction

This book is the result of an entire family's love of paper and illustration. At the turn of the century, my great-grandmother Grenell, considering colored printed ephemera a treasure, saved greeting cards, postcards, trade cards and calendars. She passed this love of printed materials on to her daughters, one of whom was my grandmother, Sylvia A. Heath, to whom this book is lovingly dedicated.

Without my dear grandma, I probably would not have begun this project. Years ago, knowing that I shared her fascination for the small spot illustrations from old magazines, she gave me envelopes filled with the little pictures she had clipped from various publications, all neatly categorized—children, women, animals, flowers, etc. I happily continued adding to this collection as I bought magazines dating from the mid-1800s to the 1950s. Helen Heath Johnson, my mother, has shared her own collection of old magazines with me to add variety to this project.

The bulk of the spot illustrations reproduced here come from the period 1915–30, although there is a smattering of cuts from 1910–14 and the early 1930s to allow for a more complete representation of trends. Silhouettes, for example, enjoyed considerable popularity from about 1928 to 1934, appearing in women's, children's and even farm and business magazines. (My grandmother and I were especially fascinated by these silhouettes, and tried our own variations in cutting them.)

Many talented artists created these spots, page decorations, fillers and ad cuts. Their charming work gave pleasure to even the most casual reader flipping through a magazine's pages, and added extra meaning to the articles and stories they graced. I am always impressed by the professionalism, aptness of detail, technical accuracy and clever styles of the art shown on these pages. Astounding in their variety and inventiveness of design and use are the borders, reverse silhouettes, vignettes, line and texture—all executed in black and white. Some pieces, enlarged, would merit fine framing and display on a wall.

I am delighted to reintroduce these marvelous illustrations to today's newsletter publishers, menu designers, craftspeople and layout artists—to all those who, like my family of "paper nuts," share a love of paper and design.

Judy M. Johnson

SPRING MILLINERY

THE DRESSING TABLE

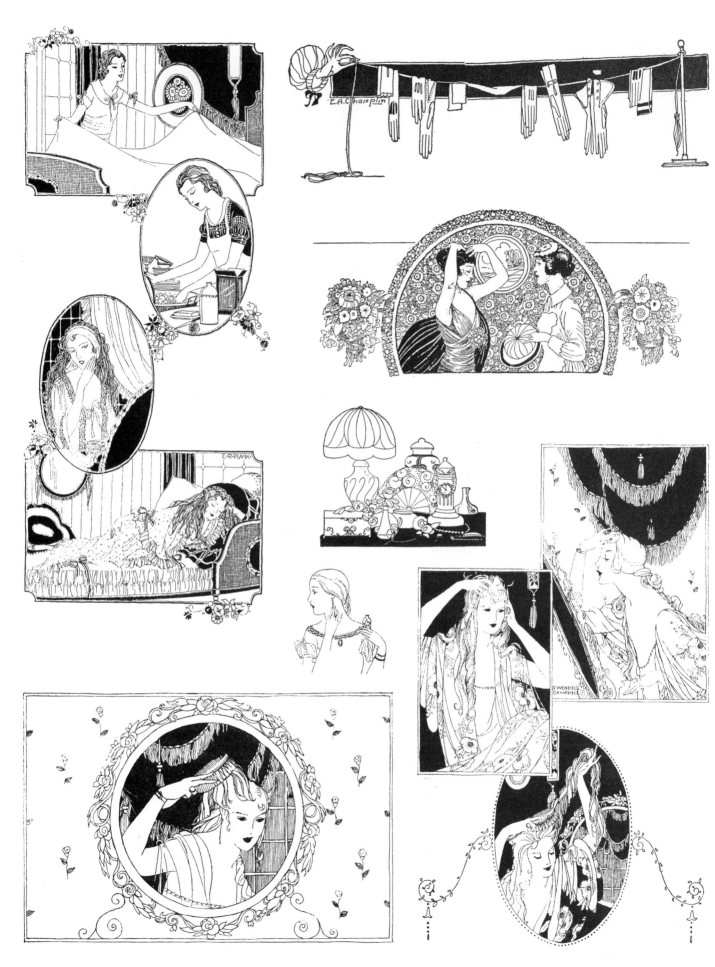

The Love Letter

The Answer

FROCKS FRILLS & FURBELOWS

A GLANCE AHEAD

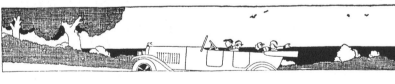

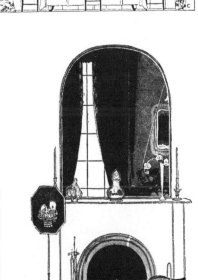

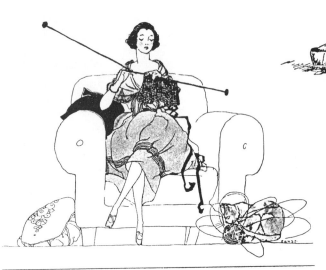

SOME STITCHERY

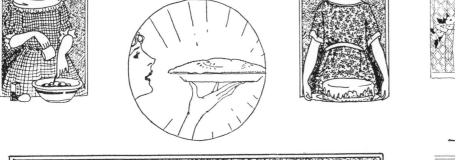

HEALTH & NUTRITION

Prize Recipes

MATTERS MUSICAL

CHRISTMAS

CHRISTMAS

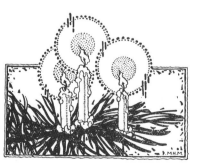

A CHRISTMAS GARLAND